How the East Wa

The Development of Football in the Eastern

CW00459322

Robert Exley

Contents

THE London UPSTART WEB

http://londonupstart.blogspot.co.uk

https://twitter.com/robert_exley

Introduction

The summer of 2012 was a period of great sporting excitement and optimism for the East quarter of London's great Metropolis. Not only had the world's largest multi-sports event taken place in Stratford, but hopeful future tenants of the Olympic Stadium – West Ham United - returned to the top flight after a years' absence. In the public's imagination 'Wess Tam' are very much the pride of East London. All major fictional Cockneys from Alf Garnett to virtually everyone from Eastenders barring Arthur Fowler (did Walford Town FC go into administration following his death in 1996?) have been decked out in the claret and blue in order to portray the authentic cockney experience to the wider viewing public. The east of the capital however has a more varied footballing history than public imagination would perceive. Though West Ham are - with all due respect to Leyton Orient – currently the biggest fish in the east end pond, few people would be aware that even the title of the most historically successful club in East London doesn't necessarily belong at the Boleyn Ground. On what we now define as 'West Ham territory' and in areas that in contemporary times we define as solidly working class there lies a Footballing Pre-history that was virtually the polar opposite.

This book will look into the inception of Football in East London, starting with the former public schoolboy 'Gentleman' amateurs of the 1870s, the game being taken up by the industrial workers of the following decade during their leisure time, the birth of professional football in the Eastern quarter of London at the end of the nineteenth century, how Football developed into a commercial enterprise at the start of the twentieth century and how football followed the Eastenders out to the Essex suburbs as the twentieth century progressed.

The clubs this book features are, among others the Forest FC, The Wanderers, Upton Park FC, Clapton, Old Castle Swifts, Thames Ironworks, West Ham United, Millwall, Arsenal (not an East End side, however their movements and actions are very important to the story of, and the development of East End football), Leyton Orient, Thames Association FC, Hornchurch FC, Ford United, Redbridge FC, Dagenham & Redbridge and their predecessor sides of Walthamstow Avenue, Leytonstone, Ilford, Dagenham FC and Redbridge Forest.

Also, 2013 is the year of the 150th anniversary of organised Football. The Football Association – the world's first such organisation and hence why they have also never felt the need to prefix the name of their nation like all other national associations - was founded at the Freemasons' Tavern near Covent Garden on 26 October 1863. Playing a very prominent role in its inception were Charles Alcock and his Leytonstone based club, Forest F.C. This story therefore also gives a very important insight into how our national game developed in modern times and became, in this secular era, the national religion – and in turn went on to conquer the world. We now proceed to the opening chapter for Football in the East of London, where it all began in the not so swinging 1860s.

Chapter One – A Class Apart

Football is of course an English folk game that goes back many centuries, with a history of several medieval monarchs trying to outlaw the pastime due the resulting disorder it brought wherever it was played. However by the time of the industrial revolution it had pretty much died out among the masses due to the 15 hour plus working days that many had to endure. By the mid-nineteenth century sporting endeavour had become the preserve of those with the luxury of leisure time – mainly former public schoolboys carrying on the games they played during their days in education. In 1863 at the Freemasons Tavern in Great Queen Street, a group of whom had come together to draw up the first set of codified rules for the game and would later go on to form the Football Association. Of the original twelve founder clubs, one had been Forest FC of Leytonstone – just two tube stops on the Central line from the Olympic Stadium in Stratford. They were formed in 1859 by Charles Alcock (pictured above) – the son of a wealthy Shipbroker who described Forest as 'the first club to work on the definite basis with the distinct object of circulating and popularising the game'. They were one of the earliest Football clubs, formed just two years after the World's oldest side - Sheffield FC.

Alcock went on to be recognised as the 'father of modern sport' due to also being involved in the Cricketing world. Alcock had turned out for Middlesex, Essex, the MCC and also served as the Secretary at Surrey County Cricket Club. He is also credited with arranging the first Cricketing test match to be played anywhere in the world – between England and Australia at Kennington Oval in 1880. He was also an esteemed Sporting journalist, working for such publications as 'The Field', 'The Sportsman', 'Football Annual', as well as editing a Cricket Newspaper for over 25 years. As a Footballer, standing at over six feet tall and weighing in at fourteen stone, his style was described as 'robust'. In his Footballing capacity, he had also devised the FA Cup - first played out among the FA's 15 member clubs in 1871/72. The idea was based on the Harrow House Football competition – the winner of which is bestowed the title of 'Cock House'.

Alcock was himself a former pupil of the famous English Public School. Forest FC by this point had changed their name to 'The Wanderers' and had won the inaugural competition by beating the Royal Engineers 1-0 at the Oval. The Wanderers had won five of the first seven FA Cups – a competition which West Ham United in contrast have only managed to win three times in their history. The star player of the Wanderers side had been Lord Kinnaird, who had won three winners medals with the side, before winning another two with the Old Etonians. In 1879 he became the first player to win the FA Cup in successive years with two different sides – a feat only ever matched by Brian Talbot exactly 100 years later with Ipswich and Arsenal. He has also appeared in nine FA Cup finals – more than any other player, including Ashley Cole. However Stepney-born Cole with seven winners' medals had surpassed Kinnaird's previous record of five in 2010, which had previously stood for 128 years prior.

However 'great' a player like Lord Kinnaird had been though, it needs to be seen within in the context of the fact that these early FA Cup competitions had been greatly restricted in terms of those who competed – in both the number of teams competing and the sections of society from which the participants had hailed from. By the end of the 1870s the Wanderers, as their name suggests, had no real fixed abode and by this time had played the majority of their games at the Oval at Kennington in Surrey. In their absence, the main side in East London by the start of 1880s had been Upton Park FC – who despite their name had borne no relation to West Ham United whatsoever.

As with Leytonstone, though Upton Park is today seen as a predominantly working class area, in the 1880s it was inhabited by those who would be described as the 'well to do' and the 'professional classes'. The area was semi-rural and mainly untouched by the urbanisation and industrialisation which affected the mainly working class areas of East London at the time. The proletarian East End had been mainly concentrated in the inner East which bordered the City of London – mainly Bethnal Green and Stepney – and the southern parts near the Dock areas, such as the Isle of Dogs and Canning Town.

Upton Park, like Forest FC, were exclusively made up of former public schoolboys who earned their daily living in professions such as the law, stockbroking, accountancy and the clergy. The possibility of someone from the Docks or the Shipyards turning out for Upton Park FC was at this time unconsidered. They even had Charles Alcock turning out for them at one point and had played their home matches in a roped off area of West Ham Park. Upton Park was also a devoutly amateur outfit with a strong belief in 'muscular Christianity', to whom the very idea of Professional football had been abhorrent.

It has also been suggested in some quarters that Upton Park FC had an aversion to 'spectatorism' and had moved from playing their matches at West Ham Park to Wanstead due to their dislike of the size of the crowds that turned out to watch them, as well as the social class make-up of the attendees. I have seen no tangible evidence to directly back this theory up, though Richard Sanders in his book 'Beastly Fury: The Strange Birth of British Football' had claimed that 'The hunched-shouldered, chain-smoking crowds who passively watched Professionals playing in Lancashire were the antithesis of the muscular Christian ideal. Many Southern clubs took positive pride from the fact that no one turned up to watch them'. These matters came to a head when Upton Park inadvertently played a part in the legalisation of Professional Football, due to a furore caused from their 4th Round FA Cup away tie at Preston North End in January 1884.

In front of a 10,000 crowd at Deepdale the game, which had been dominated by Preston, had ended 1-1 with two supposedly valid goals disallowed. The following morning Preston's club Chairman, William Sudell, had received a letter from FA Chairman Charles Alcock notifying them that a protest had been lodged against them from Upton Park FC alleging that they had breached FA rules with regard to the payment of players. Sudell was a factory owner who often employed Scottish players at his plant to purely to entice them south of the border to play for Preston. He admitted that payment was made to players, but that the practice had been widespread among sides at the time – particularly in the North of England. The FA disagreed and expelled Preston from the FA Cup for one year. Upton Park had denied lodging such a complaint, even expressing regret that the matter had been raised before the FA. From the official inquiry that arose it had been clear that a leading FA official – Nicholas 'Pa' Lane-Jackson, had been busy collecting evidence from Scotland long before the Upton Park tie.

A staunch enemy of professionalism throughout the latter years of the nineteenth century, Lane-Jackson's mentality was clearly outlined by Richard Sanders: 'For him, a hierarchy with amateurs at the top and professionals at the bottom was built into the system and unquestioned'. He was also the founder of the famous amateur side, the Corinthians – whose sole purpose was to build a side capable of matching the professionals, and who had built up a strong rivalry with Preston's professionals during the mid-1880s, who around this period had faced each other nineteen times on the pitch. Preston North End by this time were on their way to building their reputation as the 'invincibles', which came to a head by the close of the decade by winning the double in their unbeaten 1888/89 season. Their growing supremacy had begun to stick in the craw for some of the 'gentlemen' amateurs of the South.

As a result of Preston's expulsion Sudell, along with 25 other rebel clubs – mainly from outside London and the South, which included Burnley and Bolton Wanderers - had threatened to withdraw from the FA Cup, as well as the Football Association and to create a rival 'British Football Association' which embraced professionalism. What could have occurred is something akin to what appeared in Rugby a decade later and endured for over a century, where a mainly Northern code with working class players which permitted Professionalism broke away from a mainly southern, bourgeois and amateur one.

In the end the FA backed down and permitted professionalism. Within two years, in order to create a regular stream of income, the professional sides had come together to create the Football League. Of the original twelve sides, none of whom were based South of Birmingham. Despite its legalisation, professional football had yet to encroach onto the London football scene, which was to remain staunchly amateur for little while longer. Prejudices towards the professionals remained however, as James Forrest, who became the first professional to represent England in 1885 was forced to wear a different colour Jersey to the rest of his England colleagues. In fact, the bourgeois amateurs when on international duty often travelled and dined separately from their proletarian professional colleagues, often stayed in a separate hotel and generally never socially interacted with their colleagues outside of the football field.

The original amateurs of Upton Park FC lasted until 1887 before winding up. Into the vacuum came Clapton FC, which despite their name were not based in Clapton, but in Forest Gate, by the Spotted Dog Pub in Upton Lane. Clapton were a purely amateur side of middle to upper class background, though their committee were without such a staunch class division or aversion to enterprise. The 'Tons' frequently played friendlies against northern Football League professional sides and one cited possible reason for the move to Forest Gate was to exploit their close proximity to the workers of the Great Eastern Railway employed at the nearby Stratford Works, who were their main followers. Clapton also produced Walter Tull, one of the earliest Black footballers who later went on to find fame with Tottenham Hotspur.

Upton Park was to be reformed again four years later, still amateur but not quite so socially exclusive as their last incarnation had been and lasted until 1911. Also as a Post-script to the Upton Park story - while West Ham United would later lay claim to winning the World Cup for England on account of providing all of the goal scorers and the Captain of the 1966 winning side, the reprised Upton Park FC provided the entire winning team that won Gold at the inaugural Olympic Football competition at the Paris Olympics in 1900 (below), beating a French XI provided by USFSA 4-0 in the final. In keeping with their amateur ideals however, it was a typically low key affair. The entire Paris Olympics was considered as a mere sideshow to the World Exhibition in Paris and no medals had been awarded at the time, even though the IOC had awarded them to Upton Park retrospectively. The amateur ideal however, as we shall see in Chapter Two, was to be strongly challenged and the class make-up of East London Football to change drastically during the closing decade of the nineteenth century.

Chapter TWO – The Jock-ney Rebels

The biggest change on the London footballing scene, which created a shift in the social class make up of those who participated in the game, can be traced back to two pieces of progressive parliamentary legislation twenty years apart. Successive Factory acts from the 1830s onward had begun to restrict the number of hours a day the working classes toiled, however the Factory Act of 1850 had crucially made a 5 ½ day working week the norm, by including a provision that work could not continue past 2PM on a Saturday – allowing working class men the luxury of leisure time on a Saturday afternoon, which had led to numerous Works' Football sides appearing as a result. Also, the Education Act of 1870 had for the first time created universal schooling for children between the ages of five and twelve and had integrated Sports into education - something only the Public Schools such as Harrow and Eton had done previously.

Universal education had also created a literate working class and a ready-made audience for the Sports press to promote football games to a wider audience. Football in the 1880s however, had not quite the same degree of popularity in London and the South of England compared to the North of England and Scotland. Most of the work sides that sprung up in the London area in the late nineteenth century had comprised of 'migrant' workers from these parts of the UK – particularly the Scots. Their early domination over England in international fixtures can be seen by the fact that for the first twenty years of the annual England-Scotland fixture, England had won just five to Scotland's eleven matches.

A clear example of the Scottish influence in East London Football was Millwall FC, founded as Millwall Rovers on the Isle of Dogs as a works side for the J.T. Morton's Canning and Food Processing Factory (pictured above) in 1885. Millwall is of course, now explicitly associated with South East London due to the Century that the club has spent south of the River Thames. The Millwall district however is actually situated on the Western half of the Isle of Dogs, so called because in the seventeenth century Windmills were built along the west flood bank wall of the Island. Due to the gentrification which has occurred in the area over the last quarter of a Century however, this area is now rebranded by the local real estate agents as either 'Westferry' or 'South Quay' after their respective DLR stations nearby.

The last thing a Canary Wharf banker wants associated with his luxurious new riverside pad is anything redolent of Cold Blow Lane and Harry the Dog – however, it was on land which now sits in the shadow of Canary Wharf, where the founding fathers of Millwall FC once plied their rather unglamorous trade. The J.T. Morton Company itself was founded in Aberdeen in 1849 with the purpose of supplying sailing ships with food. The company opened their London branch in 1872, naturally placed in close proximity to the London Docks and also brought with them a large contingent of Scottish workers. The Millwall Lion emblem is also a by-product of their original Scottish-ness, appropriated from Scotland's Royal Coat of Arms. The East End Football Association was also founded in November 1886, with Millwall reaching the first ever final of their senior cup competition against the London Caledonians – whose very name is another nod to the Scottish influence within London football.

Millwall's East London rivals - West Ham United - can also trace their roots to Scottish industrial migrants. One of the ancestral sides in the evolutional process that led to the Hammers' creation are Castle Swifts FC. The side played in the familiar colours of Claret and Blue are said to be the reason for why the West Ham crest contains a Castle behind the two Hammers. They were founded in 1892 by Scots Shipping Magnet, Sir Donald Currie, and had mainly consisted of the employees of the company which Currie had owned, the Castle Shipping Line, which had been a Ship repair yard on the banks of the River Lea. The Swifts had played their home games at Dunottar Park in West Ham Lane – less than half a mile from where the Olympic Stadium in Stratford now lies.

Another works' side predominantly made up of Scots, who had also showed up on the radar of the East End Football scene around the same time as Millwall's formation are Dial Square FC. This side were based at the Royal Arsenal armaments factory in Woolwich and were later to evolve into Arsenal FC. According to the club's official history, as collated by former Secretary and Manager George Allison in the 1930s, their first ever match was played south of Tiller Road on the Isle of Dogs against Eastern Wanderers on December 11th 1886. This account however has recently been challenged by Arsenal historian and creator of the Woolwich Arsenal blog, Tony Attwood. Attwood rightly points out that the official history describes that the Dial Square players had crossed the Thames by the famous Woolwich Ferry to get to the Isle of Dogs to play their first fixture. Attwood notes that, as well as working a half day Saturday, as was the norm in 1886, the Woolwich Ferry didn't even exist until 1898.

The conclusion which Atwood reaches is that with the absence of a river crossing, as well as the shortness of daylight in December, Arsenal first match on the Isle of Dogs would have been practically impossible. Atwood also points to the fact that there must have been sides in nearer proximity to Woolwich for Dial Square to have played against. In response to this however, the Arsenal Independent Supporters' Association's History Society pointed out that though the free Woolwich Ferry had not yet been in existence at this point, there had been a pay Ferry that ran from the Royal Arsenal pier to Greenwich and from there a Ferry which ran to the Southern tip of the Isle of Dogs.

Another point raised to counter Atwood is found in the book 'Iron in the Blood: Thames Ironworks, the Club that Became West Ham United', which described the manner in which games were carried out around this point, stating that: 'Throughout the last decade of the 19th Century, despite our preconceived notions of Victorian efficiency, players and officials had to suffer inconsistencies in the rail transport system. Combined with this was the fact that most amateurs were obliged to work on a Saturday morning which meant a struggle to meet certain connections with horse drawn buses and steam trains. Referees, certainly at amateur level, appear to have been given a fair degree of flexibility and left to their own judgement regarding any amendment to kick off times or for bringing the game to a conclusion. It was not unknown for a match to be turned round at half-time and the whole ninety minutes played off in one period'.

In referring to a game played between two East London sides, Castle Swifts and St Lukes, from November 1892 he states that: 'The kick-off was originally scheduled for ten minutes to three, which for a murky, late autumn day was not exactly early anyway. Even so, one player on each side failed to arrive for the start. When they did make an appearance, at different times, the referee must have decided that such interruptions were time consuming for he did not blow his whistle for half-time until nineteen minutes to four, i. e. six minutes for wasted time! Due to this decision he allowed an interval of four minutes only, so the second half began at a quarter to four, but because the light was fading badly the referee blew for time at 4.21, nine minutes short. The game was not considered abandoned and was not replayed. This was far from an isolated case'.

Therefore, bearing in mind this degree of flexibility with regards to the duration of a Match, even though the journey from Woolwich to the Isle of Dogs would have still been a time-consuming one, even with a river crossing, there still would have been sufficient time left over for a Football match of sorts to have been carried out. There were also numerous recorded instances of matches from this period where Arsenal had played other East End sides - particularly Millwall. Therefore the link of contacts within the Scottish diaspora may well have overridden Geography when considering which sides the Arsenal's founding fathers were to play.

Even though Arsenal were a South London outfit at this point, they were responsible for the most important paradigm shift to affect East London Football. Their 1891 FA Cup tie against Professional side Derby County had resulted in the opposition poaching two of the Arsenal's star players by offering them professional terms. In response Royal Arsenal - as they were known at this point - decided to openly embrace professionalism. They were at this point the first side in London to actually do so. It was a move however that was to see them expelled from the London FA as a result, due to the dominance of the Upper and Middle Class Amateurs within the organisation at the time – particularly Nicholas 'Pa' Lane-Jackson of the Corinthians, who had tried but ultimately failed to stop Preston North End and the Professional game developing in the North around a decade earlier. Several sides in the London area – Particularly Millwall and Tottenham Hotspur - were now attracting sizeable crowds and were also keen to Professionalise, however were unwilling to face the kind of ostracising sanctions which the Arsenal were now subjected to as a result.

One of the routes that Royal Arsenal had sought around the dilemma that was created by expulsion from the London FA was to plan a Southern equivalent of the predominantly northern Football League - which had been formed in 1888 – to generate the revenue to make Professional Football in London and the South a viable enterprise. Arsenal however eventually entered the Football League, as the first side south of Birmingham to do so and effectively making it a national league. However, few of the other sides in the London area at this point were inclined to take on the extra costs involved in travelling the rest of the country. Instead they pursued Arsenal's original idea, by forming the Southern League – of which Millwall had been the prime movers to create, as well as becoming the inaugural winners in 1894/95, retaining their title twelve months later and then coming runners up the following season in 1896/97.

The Southern League was a commercially successful enterprise and the London sides involved – particularly Millwall and Tottenham Hotspur - drew larger attendances than what the Arsenal, now renamed as Woolwich Arsenal - could muster in the Football League around the same period. In 1894, looking to capitalise on the growing trend for local workers to spend their Saturday afternoons at the Football, Sir Donald Currie was to merge his Castle Swifts FC with another local side, Old St Lukes – and in the process forming Old Castle Swifts FC. They moved to Old St. Luke's former ground in Canning Town, closer to the Shipyard of the Castle Line, from where the club would draw most of its support. Old Castle Swifts however were only to last one season.

They were one of the earliest professional sides in the East London area; however such a venture in further Eastern regions of London's urban sprawl was yet to be a commercially viable one. Sir Donald Currie was no longer inclined to bankroll the club and so the team folded at the end of the 1894/95 season. The void left by Currie however, was to be almost immediately filled within a month by another cash rich benefactor in the shape of Arnold Hills, the owner of the Thames Ironworks & Shipbuilding company, who were situated on the banks opposite the Castle Ship repair yard on the River Lea.

While in attendance at the 1895 FA Cup Final at Crystal Palace with his foreman David Taylor, the latter had suggested to Hills that the Company should form its own Football team. Oddly enough, Hills was a former footballer himself, having played for Oxford University in the 1877 FA Cup Final and had represented England at international level. One notable game which Hills took part in is the 5-4 defeat of Scotland at the Oval; the only win for an England side mainly made up of former public school boys, against the Auld Enemy between 1873 and 1888. As irony would have it, Hills's formation of the Thames Ironworks' side was also to be a direct challenge to Scots domination over the East London Football scene.

The newly formed Thames Ironworks FC took over the tenancy at Old Castle Swifts former ground at Hermit Road in Canning Town, as well as signing four of their now redundant former players. And even though on the playing side, East London football was firmly established as a working class game, with the introduction of Arnold Hills to the East London football scene, control over its direction had swung firmly back in the direction of the Old Harrovian public schoolboys, just as it had been around a quarter of a century earlier with Charles Alcock and Forest FC. The battle between the 'Gentlemen' amateur ideals and proletarian led professionalism however was far from over, as will be seen in Chapter three.

The Thames Ironworks and Shipbuilding Company were founded in 1846 and by the 1860s had been the biggest shipbuilders on the Thames, employing around 6000 people. By the close of the nineteenth century however the Shipyards saw a decline in fortune, due to the cost advantages of yards in the North East of England and Clydeside in Glasgow with closer supplies of coal and iron. By 1895 the number of men employed at the Ironworks had dwindled to around 3000. A controlling interest in the Ironworks was bought by successful industrial chemist and entrepreneur Frank Clarke Hills in 1871. In 1880 his twenty three year old son, Arnold Hills, had joined the board, eventually taking full control of the firm upon his father death in 1893. Among the superlatives used to describe Arnold Hills have been 'paternalistic philanthropist' and a 'gentleman capitalist', he even chose to live among his workforce in a small house in the East India Dock Road in Canning Town for a number of years.

Hills however for most of the early 1890s had been embroiled in a series of bitter industrial disputes with the employees of the Ironworks, the roots of which dated back to the Great London Dock Strike of 1889. The Great Strike had centred on the pay and conditions of the Dock workers - mainly the demands of four hours continuous work at a time and a minimum rate of sixpence an hour. Up to 10,000 men went out on strike and after five weeks the employers accepted defeat, conceding to most of the demands of the workers. After the strike, the Dockers went on to organise the General Labourers' Union – in London alone 20,000 workers went on to join the Union. The Great Strike of 1889 had affected the Thames Ironworks quite badly, even after the matter was resolved for the rest of the Docklands. Industrial unrest at the Ironworks had spread well into 1890 and 1891 with joiners and engineers going out on strike. The firm had then created a great deal of bad feeling by sacking these workers and employing non-unionised labour in their place.

Hills however had wanted to ease the tense relations that were a hang-over from the Great Strike and in 1892 he created the 'Good Fellowship scheme' of bonuses on top of standard wage rates. In 1894 he introduced an eight hour day for his workers – one of the first to do so voluntarily, at a time when ten and twelve hour shifts were the norm in industrial work. He also introduced the Thames Ironworks' Quarterly Gazette as a mode of communication with his workforce, which has since been described as part local newspaper, part corporate propaganda. The paper had also advertised corporate facilities, such as the workers' clubs Hills had set up himself, which included activities such as Cricket, Rowing, Athletics, Cycling, a string band, a drama group, an operatic society and even a debating society. It was also through the Gazette that the idea of a works' football side was first announced under the headline: 'The importance of co-operation between workers and management'. It was obvious that Hills had felt that bankrolling a works' side would help heal the divisions between him and his workforce.

A Thames Ironworks side also may well have fitted in with the 'Muscular Christianity' that Hills was taught from his days at the Harrow Public School. Arnold Hills was also a prominent member of the Temperance Society and even at one point had only wanted teetotallers turning out for the Ironworks' side. The Irons were also an extension of his social conscience and concern for the locals, having stated that 'the lack of recreational facilities was one of the worst deprivations in the lives of West Ham residents'. Hills's biography on the website of the Oxford University A.F.C. states that: 'there were few green spaces in West Ham, so most young men played football in the spaces between factories. Hills saw this local problem as directly related to local issues such as 'bands of young hooligans' on the streets'.

However, unlike their predecessor side, Old Castle Swifts, Hills was adamant that the Ironworks' side was not to embrace professionalism, which was no doubt a hang-over from Hills's days as a sporting amateur. He was also critical of the Irons' decision that their governing committee should consist of non-players, as well as the recruitment of top coaches and top playing staff, the club's decision to compete in the FA Cup and the introduction of player's insurance to cover loss of earnings resulting from injury. The Oxford University A.F.C. website elaborates by stating that the idea of professionalism 'was anathema to Hills, for whom sport was an end in itself and should exhibit Corinthian values', but also 'the irony was that, by acting as a wealthy benefactor, Hills gave Thames Ironworks FC an advantage over more established clubs'.

The club also had no such aversion to 'spectatorism' as previous amateur sides had and even pioneered floodlit football in their first season with a friendly with Woolwich Arsenal in December 1895. It was reported in the Gazette that 'the occasion was a success...ten lights each of 2,000 candle power gave a good view to those present'. The club were also later to be evicted from their home at Hermit Road for breaching their tenancy agreement by charging admission fees, as well as building a perimeter fence and a pavilion. Hills then decided to stump up £20,000 of his own funds to acquire the land to build the Memorial Grounds which opened on the day of Queen Victoria's Diamond Jubilee in 1897. The ground was situated close to where West Ham station now stands.

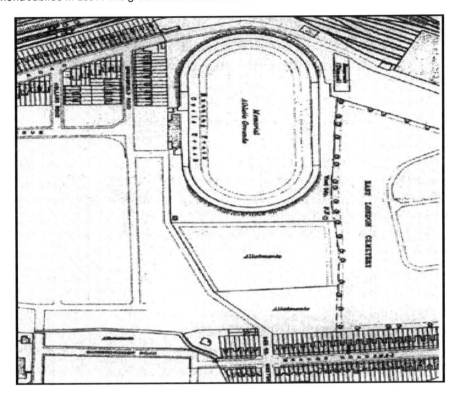

Hills had hoped for the Stadium (above) to hold a capacity of 133,000 and to host future FA Cup Finals – applications were made by Hills but none granted by the FA. He had also planned for the grounds to contain the largest outdoor Swimming Pool in England, Tennis Courts and was also to host Cycling and Athletics meetings – kind of a mini East London Olympic village 115 years early if you will. Thames Ironworks F.C. however had failed to attract the crowds to the Memorial Grounds, averaging just around the 2,000 mark, which had meant that the club was being run at a loss and reliant on the funds of Arnold Hills to survive.

In a bid to attract larger crowds the club eventually did turn professional at the start of the 1898/99 season to attract a better standard of players and also joined the Southern League Division Two, of which they easily won by finishing nine points ahead of their nearest rivals under a two points for a win system. This new professionalism however didn't sit well with Hills, stating that 'the committees of several of our clubs, eager for immediate success, are inclined to reinforce their ranks with mercenaries. In our bands and in our football clubs, I find an increasing number of professionals who do not belong to our community but are paid to represent us in their several capacities'.

By the dawn of the twentieth century Arnold Hills had looked to expand his business interests by acquiring the Engineering firm John Penn and Sons and amalgamating the firm with his own. In order to raise new funds, a new public company was formed under the name of the Thames

Ironworks Shipbuilding and Engineering Company, which made Hills accountable to shareholders for how he utilised the firm's funds and hence, was unable to continue bankrolling the Ironworks' Football side. As a result, the side were therefore to dissolve its ties with the Company and Thames Ironworks FC were officially wound up in June 1900 and immediately reformed as West Ham United – whom had taken the spot left vacant by Thames Ironworks in the Southern League.

The amalgamation with John Penn and Sons however turned out to be a bad business move for Hills, leading to a serious decline in fortune for the Thames Ironworks, which ultimately ended in the Ironworks' closure in 1912. As a result of his dwindling finances, by 1904 Hills was unwilling to re-negotiate a rental agreement for West Ham United to use the Memorial Grounds, meaning that the club were required to seek a new home, which they ultimately found at the Boleyn Castle Field off of Green Street in Upton Park. The change of location for the Hammers however had caused no identity crisis in the way that Woolwich Arsenal or Millwall had done on their respective moves due to the fact that the eastern boundary of the West Ham County Borough had been Green Street itself and had remained that way until the boundaries were redrawn with the creation of the GLC in 1965.

The idea of naming the club Upton Park after its new location would also have caused some confusion due to the two previous Upton Park clubs that existed in the late nineteenth century. The only subsequent confusion arising from the move would have been for away fans using the District Line, as to whether West Ham or Upton Park would have been the correct destination for the Boleyn Ground. The move however ultimately turned out to be a profitable one for the Hammers and initially so for reasons oddly similar to the demographics of football attendance today. According to Dave Russell in his book 'Football and the English: A Social History of Association Football in England' at around the dawn of the twentieth century "in terms of social class, crowds at Football League matches were predominantly drawn from the skilled working and lower-middle classes... Social groups below that level were largely excluded by the admission price, quite possibly in a deliberate attempt to limit the access of poorer (and supposedly "rowdier") supporters'.

Your average skilled tradesmen's wage around this time was usually less than £2 a week. Tickets for your average football game involving professional sides at the start of the twentieth century in comparison had cost around 4 pence, whereas admission fee for the local musical hall or the cinema was around 3 pence. Upton Park at this time was still a fairly salubrious part of the world, especially in comparison to the Canning Town area that the Hammers had left behind. By the end of their first full season at the Boleyn Ground in 1904/05, the club had turned an £800 loss into a £400 profit and increased gate receipts from £2,900 to £4,300 in the process - and, of course, have remained in the Upton Park area to this very day. Within a decade of West Ham's move however, there would be further relocations of other clubs that would mould the geography of London Football as we now know it today. A process of which, in Chapter 4 we will divulge a little further.

Chapter 4 – The Wandering Tribes of East End Football

Though the Lion's Den is now situated in Bermondsey, south of the Thames, for the first 25 years of their existence Millwall had played at four different sites on the Isle of Dogs in the East End of London. Also, where the formation of their rivals - West Ham - was very much centred on the teetotalism of Arnold Hills and his wish to save the working man from drink related ruin; the public houses of the Isle of Dogs and their patrons played a central role in Millwall's formation and early sustenance. Their first pitch in 1885 had been an unenclosed patch of land near Tiller Road – quite possibly the very same one in which Arsenal were claimed to have played their first ever game a year later. The Islander Pub at Tooke Street, known locally as 'Sextons' after its landlord, acted as the club's first HQ, as well as their changing rooms, for their time at Glengall Road. Jesper Sexton, the seventeen year old son of the Islander's landlord Maurice Sexton, had also acted as the club's first secretary.

The Islander pub now no longer exists, having been destroyed by the Luftwaffe during the Blitz in September 1940 and never rebuilt, however the Public House to which Millwall had later relocated to the rear of by the start of their second season - the Lord Nelson Pub (above) at East Ferry Road - still exists to this very day. The club had remained there for four years until they were evicted by the pub's landlady in 1890. Their final game at the Lord Nelson had been a benefit game against the Royal Arsenal, the proceeds of which paid for their new home – the Athletic Ground – which had been Millwall's first purpose build stadium, holding up to 20,000 people. The ground had been situated near to the George Public house – another pub still which still stands on the Isle of Dogs today. The club benefitted from the Athletic Grounds' close proximity to Millwall Dock Station, on the Millwall extension line of the London and Blackwall Railway Company line – a line which fell into disuse by the early twentieth century but later revived in the 1980s as the Docklands Light Railway, with Crossharbour station now standing where Millwall Docks previously had done.

The land on which the Athletic Ground stood however had belonged to the Millwall Docks Company, who in 1901 had wanted to commandeer it to build a timber yard. Millwall therefore were required to move again, this time to an area which at this point was referred to as 'North Greenwich' – a name which now refers to the tube station nearest to the 02 Arena, however at this point referred to the area between where now stands between the Mudchute and Island Gardens DLR stations. Their attendances at North Greenwich however had dwindled to around an average of 6,000, mainly because unlike the Athletic ground the area was ill served by public transport.

The club therefore looked to south of the river for the solution, believing that the density of population in the Bermondsey and New Cross areas in comparison to the Isle of Dogs would be fertile breeding ground for larger gate receipts. Also, transport links between the East End and South East London had greatly improved with the opening of the Greenwich Foot tunnel in 1902, which was built with the intention of enabling workers living on the south side of the Thames to reach their workplaces in the docks on the North Side of the river. This was followed by the opening of the Rotherhithe tunnel in 1908 which connected Limehouse to Rotherhithe by road.

Both of these had complimented the existing rail link between Wapping and New Cross via Isambard Kingdom Brunel's Thames Tunnel. Millwall therefore took the decision in 1910 to relocate to Cold Blow Lane in New Cross, though obviously hoped to retain their existing fan base north of the river by keeping the name which referred to their original stomping ground and a prominent Lions contingent had remained in the E14 and E1 postcodes throughout the twentieth century. Millwall's arrival south of the river that year however had no doubt set alarm bells ringing further along the southern bank of the Thames at Woolwich.

The Arsenal were under severe financial pressure and no doubt would not have relished another side narrowing their patch for a potential fan base. At that time Bermondsey had been 40 minutes nearer to Central London than Arsenal's base at Plumstead. In Woolwich itself, the Royal Arsenal had considerably downsized its workforce which hence, had a large impact on the club's attendances that had dwindled to as low as 3,000 by the end of their time in Plumstead in the 1912/13 season. The club was in such a financial predicament that the original limited company set up when the club turned professional in 1893 was dissolved and a new company was brought into existence.

The club was bought up by Sir Henry Norris in 1910, who had initially wanted to merge the club with Fulham, but the Football League refused to sanction the plan. Norris had promised to keep the club in Plumstead for two years, however after this time had elapsed had moved the club to the Highbury area of North London, with the added benefit of being close to the Piccadilly Line station of Gillespie Road and its direct links with the West End of London. Arsenal's move brought staunch opposition from Chelsea and Tottenham Hotspur, who had accused the Woolwich 'interlopers' of stealing their patch.

The move also however had an effect on the eastern half of the metropolis, due to the Highbury's close proximity to parts of the east end which lay close to the North of London, such as Hackney and Clapton or bordered on the City of London, such as Bethnal Green. One such club affected by the move had been London's second oldest Football club, Clapton Orient. The club were founded by the Glyn Cricket Club who were based near Homerton in 1881, as a way of keeping fit during the winter months. By 1901 they had moved to Millfields Stadium, where they would stay for another three decades.

The chairman of the Orient supporters club, Steve Jenkins, claimed that 'Orient were on a par with Arsenal and Tottenham before the war...But with Arsenal moving north of the river from Woolwich the population couldn't sustain three clubs of that size'. Jenkins's point however is a little overstated, as Pre-1913 Orient were firmly rooted in the lower of the two divisions that existed at the time, where Arsenal prior to their only ever relegation in 1913 had spent nine consecutive seasons in the top division. Tottenham also had spent four consecutive seasons in the old Division One by 1913.

Orient had successfully applied to join the Football League in 1905; however were required to fund considerable improvements to the stadium that were needed to comply with League requirements, such as increasing the stadium capacity from 12,000 to 20,000. Orient had finished their first league season rooted to the foot of the table, this was compounded by the fact that they were only saved from being wound up by the generosity of a supporter who donated £50. Re-election had only been granted to Orient due to the fact that their chairman, Captain Henry Wells-Holland, at the League management committee hearing had played to the club's potential as the only Football League side in East London at this point (and only one of just three London Clubs in the Football League) as well as the potential of their seven acre-site at Millfields Road Stadium 'as one of the largest in Southern England and can easily be made capable of holding upwards of 60,000'.

Records of attendances at the Millfields prior to 1913 are hard to come by, however there are suggestions in many quarters that the club's far more successful Baseball side (above) had gone some way to subsidizing the Football club's existence. In 1906 several top-level Football sides, including Woolwich Arsenal, Tottenham and Derby County, had formed the British Baseball Association as way of generating revenue during the summer months. The popularity of Baseball in Clapton had been so considerable that they were National Champions for two seasons out of three between 1907 and 1909. A rare instance of the Football side turning out huge crowds had been at the end of the 1914-15 season, when 22,000 fans turned up for the visit of Leicester Fosse as a send-off for the 41 members of staff and players who had signed up en mass to join the forces fighting the Great War.

The four year break enforced on Football between 1914-18 greatly affected Orient's finances. There had also been post-war expansion of the Football League after 1919 which saw West Ham and Millwall both elected to the League and eroding Orient's East End monopoly on Football League, as well as the aforementioned two sides' proximity to the Docks which would eat up the potential attendances for Dockers seeking post-work entertainment after finishing their half-day Saturday shifts. Also, it was not so much Arsenal's arrival in North London which affected Orient's progress, but Herbert Chapman's in 1925. Orient attempted to rebuild the Millfields Stadium around the same time as Arsenal had begun to flourish in the North Eastern corner of London and, as a result had restricted their potential gate receipts.

By 1927 Orient were still greatly in debt as a result of their re-development plan and could therefore not afford to purchase the expired freehold on the Millfields Stadium from the local council. The site was eventually sold to a syndicate headed by Lady Amherst, who had intended to convert the Stadium for use as a Greyhound Racing track – later to be renamed as Clapton Stadium (Below). Also, in the late 1920s Arsenal had bought into Orient with the intention of using the club as a nursery side for the development of young players, until the FA outlawed such a practice leaving Orient in some considerable financial difficulty without Arsenal's cash injection.

Despite the intentions of the new owners of the Millfield Stadium, Clapton Orient continued to lease the ground. However the new landlords looked to coerce the tenants out, forbidding their use of the pitch for training and the extra expense that was incurred in renting a separate site elsewhere. Orient's directors were also denied the use of the board-room on match-days. By 1930 the club moved to a stadium in Lea Bridge Road, which doubled up as a Speedway arena. Due to its dual purpose, the stadium had a wooden fence around its perimeter. The Football League had received complaints that the fencing was too near to the touchline and were ordered to extend the narrow pitch.

Also, a rare large crowd of 20,000 for the visit of Millwall had also resulted in pitch invasions due to overcrowding. Orient soon became aware that the Lea Bridge Road Stadium was not fit for purpose. As a result they had used Highbury and even Wembley as a temporary solution. By 1937 they decided to ground share with cash strapped side Leyton Amateurs at Brisbane Road and have remained there ever since, changing their name to Leyton Orient in 1946. The Orient's historical subordination as a club to the interests of sports such as Baseball, Greyhound Racing and Speedway gives some insight into the kind of competition that professional football in East London faced in the first half of the twentieth century.

In 1927 the West Ham Stadium was built near Prince Regent Lane in the Custom House area and with a capacity of 120,000 was at that point the largest stadium in England. The Stadium acted as a home ground for the West Ham Speedway Side, as well as hosting Greyhound Racing. Both events took place during the week; however the Stadium owners had wanted something to generate revenue on the weekends and hence had formed Thames Association FC. It may well sound a slightly odd concept to found a side purely to fill a stadium, however this is exactly how Chelsea F.C. were formed in 1905 in order for businessmen Gus and Joe Mears, the owners of the leasehold of Stamford Bridge, to host Football games at what had been mainly an Athletics Stadium for nearly 30 years prior after Fulham had turned down their initial offer to occupy the Stadium.

THAMES ASSOCIATION F.C.   1928
West Ham Stadium, Prince Regent Lane, Custom House, London E.16

The idea of Thames Association F.C. however didn't prove to be a successful one. The side had been elected to the Football League Third Division South in 1930, however in their two seasons in the league had finished in the bottom three on both occasions. They also struggled to attract the crowds to sustain league football, averaging just 2000 fans per game and had achieved an all-time record low attendance of just 469 for their game against Luton Town in December 1930 – which is an incredibly small size crowd for a Stadium (pictured above) that was actually bigger than Wembley. After finishing rock bottom in 1931/32 the club had refrained from seeking re-election to the Football League.

They had also turned down the offer of a merger from a Clapton Orient side desperately seeking an adequate stadium and subsequently folded. The West Ham Stadium itself continued to exist for the purposes of Speedway, Greyhound Racing and later Baseball and Stock Car Racing. After the Second World War however attendances for Sports meetings – particularly the kinds of Sports which previously filled the Stadium, had dwindled due to new forms of entertainment, such as Television. West Ham Stadium eventually became obsolete and was demolished in 1972 to make way for a housing estate – and maybe after the Olympics is a timely reminder of what can happen to a previously grandiose stadium if not filled by a reasonably large Football side, with a reasonably large existing fan base, on a regular basis.

Chapter 5: The Only Way Is Essex

It was twenty years ago this August when the top flight broke away from the rest of the Football League and formed the FA Premier League and officially (well in the eyes of Sky Sports at least) created Football as we know it. One other lesser recognised twentieth anniversary however was that of one of the youngest football clubs in the whole of the top four divisions of professional football in England – Dagenham and Redbridge FC. Despite the recent nature of the Daggers' formation however, the background to their history goes back as far as the roots of Football in the Eastern hemisphere of the metropolis itself. It involved an amalgamation of three of the biggest names in Amateur Football who between them won the FA Trophy once, the FA Amateur Cup seven times, the Isthmian League twenty times, the Athenian League six times, the Essex Senior Cup twenty-six times and the London Senior Cup twenty-three times.

The story starts in 1881 in Ilford, which at this point was a mere Essex village with a population of just 7500 people, yet to be subsumed into London's great urban sprawl. It was here that a group of young men had formed Ilford Alliance FC, which was later renamed just plain Ilford FC. The club were on the forefront of early amateur football, winning the Essex Senior Cup in 1888 and were entrants to the inaugural FA Amateur Cup in 1893. They were also founder members of the Southern League when it was formed in 1894. As the Southern league was soon to become to be dominated by professional sides such as Tottenham Hotspur, Millwall and Southampton however, staunch amateurs Ilford came to be out of their depth – finishing bottom of the table with just one point in 1896. As a result of this, they had voluntarily withdrawn from the Southern League and joined the newly formed London League, which Arnold Hills of Thames Ironworks had been instrumental in establishing in order to preserve the amateur ethic within the London Footballing scene.

By 1905 the London League had merely become an outlet for many of London's professional sides to field their reserves, therefore Ilford – along with other prominent amateur sides within the London area such as Clapton FC, the Casuals and London Caledonians had formed the Isthmian League to provide a genuinely competitive Amateur Football League for sides in the London and Home

Counties area. By the 1920s Ilford had come to prominence within the amateur game by winning the FA Amateur Cup back to back in 1929 and 1930. Also playing in Isthmian League were Leytonstone FC, who were founded in 1886. By the late 1930s they had come to dominate the Isthmian League, winning the title on seven consecutive occasions between 1937 and 1951 (taking into account Football's seven year break for the Second World War). They had also won back to back FA Amateur Cups in 1947 and 1948.

The growth of amateur Football sides on the outer eastern fringe of the metropolis during the inter-war and early post-war years had coincided with population growth as a direct result of suburban expansion from house building schemes enacted by the London County Council, with 'out-county' Council Estates built in parts of West Essex – such as the Becontree and Harold Hill Estates - as part of David Lloyd-George's 'Homes Fit For Heroes' policy after the First World War. Despite not being part of London itself for at least another four decades, the West Essex fringe had been ideal for house building due to the availability of open, empty space close by which could be bought up at a cheaper price. There had also been a great expansion of private sector house building in the 1930s, which saw London's urban area expand at a rate greater than it has done before or since.

One such beneficiary of this had been Walthamstow Avenue FC. The side were formed in 1900, coinciding with the population of the town increasing ten-fold from that of just 30 years prior. The Avenue however only came to prominence after 1930, as a result of the suburban expansion which occurred in the North of Walthamstow and into nearby Chingford, of which the club with their home base at Green Pond Road were able to exploit with the aid of the tram link between the two areas. During the 1930s they had dominated the Amateur Athenian League for most of the decade. After the war they joined the Isthmian League, which they won at their first attempt and had built a reputation as one of the most feared sides in the amateur game winning the league a further three times over the next decade, as well as the FA Amateur Cup in 1952 and again in 1961.

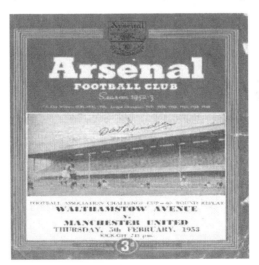

They were however most famed for their FA Cup exploits, particularly reaching the 4th Round in 1953 against Matt Busby's Manchester United, who were at this point the reigning League Champions. On the way they had disposed of league sides Stockport and Watford and heroically held United to a 1-1 draw at Old Trafford. The amateurs however were beaten 5-2 in the replay, which had been a home fixture played at nearby Highbury attracting a crowd of 49,000. The scorer of all of their three goals against United had been a future title winner with Chelsea in 1955, Jim Lewis, who as an amateur would represent Great Britain at three Olympic Games.

The Avenue's Green Pond Road ground had also been used for Football in the 1948 London Olympic Games, bringing in an attendance of 21,000 to watch Turkey v China. Ilford's Lynn Road Stadium was also used for France v India, attracting a 17,000 attendance, who were for the most part amazed that the Indian side had taken to the field barefoot. Despite this perceived handicap, it took a last minute goal from the French to eliminate India 2-1. As a result of the stir caused by this game, FIFA had outlawed playing barefoot at the 1950 World Cup Finals, which was cited as a reason for India's withdrawal despite having qualified for the tournament.

The final side involved in the story of the Daggers' pre-history are Dagenham FC, who were founded as late as 1949. The club were formed on the back of the rapid growth of the town in light of the construction of the Becontree Estate which started in 1921. At the time it was – and in fact still remains – the largest public housing development in the world. This saw a ten-fold increase in the areas population within ten years, which was followed by the opening of the nearby Ford Motor Works site in 1931. Dagenham FC had reached back to back FA Amateur Cup Finals in 1970 and 1971, however losing on both occasions. Within a few years the Amateur Cup was to be abolished and replaced by the FA Trophy, of which Dagenham reached the final of in 1977, however, were to be beaten finalists again that year.

Until the late 1970s, all four sides – Leytonstone, Ilford, Walthamstow Avenue and Dagenham – were four separate independent Footballing entities. However in 1977, due to financial difficulties Ilford FC were forced to sell Lynn Road Stadium to Fairview Homes, who in turn built a housing development on the site. Just three years prior Ilford had reached the last ever FA Amateur Cup Final before its abolition, of which they lost to fellow Essex side Bishop Stortford 4-1. The club had bought a site to build a new ground, on land which had been a former RAF airfield in Fairlop. However after tax deductions they were not left with enough funds from the original proceeds of the sale of Lynn Road to re-develop the site. In the meantime they were tenants of Leytonstone FC, before deciding to merge with the club in 1979 to form Leytonstone & Ilford FC. Initially a success, the side were Isthmian League Champions in 1982 and Runners Up the following year; however by 1985 they were running at a considerable loss and themselves were forced to sell their ground at Granleigh Road and ground share with Walthamstow Avenue at Green Pond Lane.

By 1988 Walthamstow Avenue were 'incorporated' into Leytonstone & Ilford, who in turn won the Isthmian League the following season but were denied entry to the Conference League as their ground was not deemed fit for purpose and were forced to relocate to Victoria Road to ground share with Dagenham FC. The club had in the meantime found a site for a new ground and thus changed their name to Redbridge Forest FC after their chosen new home area on the borders of the London Boroughs of Redbridge and Waltham Forest. The move however fell through, leaving the club stuck at Victoria Road. Redbridge Forest were crowned Isthmian League Champions in 1991 and as Dagenham's Victoria Road Stadium was suitable for Conference level Football, coupled with Dagenham's financial turmoil, a decision was reached to merge the two sides for the 1992/93 season.

The decision however was not universally popular with fans of Dagenham FC, as seen from Derek Robinson's article in When Saturday Comes magazine in July 1992, claiming that: 'with the committees of both clubs having shown a complete inability to handle money, I give Dagenham & Redbridge FC five years at the most......And that's being generous'. The club however have long since survived and thrived – achieving both financial stability and a place in the Football League as a result. The club however are not particularly popular with the Football purists. In 2007, their Conference League fixture with fellow merger created side Rushden & Diamonds was the subject of David Stubb's When Saturday Comes article, which referred to the match as 'a case of Pariah v Pariah'.

Stubb's article also further states that 'the whole business of mergers is not just confusing and depressing, but a source of some bitterness to other Conference fans in particular – the lower leagues, far from being gentler pastures of homelier, more authentic footballing culture, would seem to be more vulnerable to these sorts of dealings and enforced uprootings. Such amalgamations remind me of 1970s comics, when Tiger "merged" with Jag'. Much of this dislike however is largely lost on the Daggers, as 'among the Dagenham fans....or even among the websites, it's hard to gauge any particular mood of defensiveness or siege mentality. They seem oblivious to that – a case of "no one likes us, we don't know".

Dagenham and Redbridge however are not to be confused with another similarly named side operating out on the far Eastern fringe of London's urban sprawl – Redbridge F.C. – despite a few shared similarities, such as their creation through a merger between two separate sides previously based in Dagenham - one of whom were based at the Daggers current home of Victoria Road. Until 2004 they had been known as Ford United FC, who were created by a merger in 1958 between Dagenham based sides Ford Sports and Brigg Sports – the latter had even reached an FA Amateur Cup Semi-final in 1954 against Bishop Auckland, which was played in front of a 58,000 crowd at St. James' Park, Newcastle. The newly formed club had longstanding links with the giant Motor Corporation which bore its name, having played their home games at the Ford Sports Ground in Romford until 2000, when the Ford Motor Company refused to grant anything other than a yearly lease of the venue to the club – something which Isthmian League rules had not permitted. The club then moved to the Oakside Stadium (below), a ground which was shared with Barkingside FC in the borough of Redbridge.

In 2004, despite being as high as the sixth tier of English Football, Ford United had an average attendance of only 150, of which the club attributed to a lack of geographical reference point within their chosen moniker. Therefore the decision had been made to rename themselves as Redbridge FC in order to ingratiate themselves with the local population. Dagenham and Redbridge objected to the name switch, insisting that they were 'not happy about another team taking half of their name and will be making their feelings known to the Football Association'. Their protest however fell on deaf ears, largely because unlike the Daggers, Ford United were actually resident within the Borough of Redbridge. However their attempts to further their fan base have largely been dashed by two successive relegations from the Conference South to Ryman League Division One North, where Redbridge FC now currently resides.

Around the same period in which Ford United were 'stealing' their name, a local rivalry had also built up between Dagenham and Redbridge and Hornchurch FC, due to the fact that the latter had poached several ex-Daggers players and manager Garry Hill. Their free spending habits had saw them dubbed the 'Chelsea of the non-league' and saw the club rise from Division Three of the Ryman League to the top of the Conference South within a few short years. They were reported to have a playing budget of £1.2 Million, despite having only average gate receipts of around £30,000 per season. However, their financial benefactor, the Double Glazing firm Carthium Group, incurred over £7 Million of debt and went bust, and along with it so too did Hornchurch FC in 2004. Therefore any threat posed to the Daggers by their upstart neighbours – be they poaching the club's name or personnel – turned out to be minimal seeing that the club rose up into the Football League and reached as high as the third tier of English Football by the close of the decade.

Despite sinking back down to just six points off the drop back to the Conference in 2011/2012, the Daggers now start their sixth consecutive season in the Football league and rather than looking to non-league Hornchurch or Redbridge for rivalry, it's the more established Football League opposition of Southend United and Barnet that provide the Daggers main source of rivalry for the 2012/13 season. And if anything, finally indicates a rare era of stability for a Footballing entity which has shape-shifted and its way through non-league Football throughout the decades.

Printed in Great Britain
by Amazon